95p 50p

Lifelines 42

GW00750877

Vanbrugh

An illustrated life of Sir John Vanbrugh

1664-1726

John Anthony

Shire Publications Ltd

Contents

ACKNOWLEDGEMENTS

The author wishes to thank the following for assistance in preparing this book: Mr R. Farquarson at Eastbury, Mr J. W. F. Cole at Claremont, Mr W. P. Jones and Mr M. V. Morton at Vanbrugh Castle, the Earl of Ancaster at Grimsthorpe Castle, and the staff of the police training school at Kings Weston.

Illustrations are acknowledged as follows: John Anthony, pages 4, 16, 17 (bottom), 21, 23, 24, 28 (both), 31 (top right), 34, 37 (both), 40, 41, 44, 45; Bodleian Library, Oxford, page 43; British Library Board, page 31 (bottom); Castle Howard Estates, page 14, cover; Chichester Festival Theatre, page 10; National Monuments Record, page 12; National Portrait Gallery, pages 2, 27; Sir John Soane's Musuem, page 18; Victoria and Albert Museum, Crown Copyright, pages 9, 17 (top), 31 (top left).

The cover shows an engraving of the scheme for Castle Howard as published in 1725. See also page 14.

Printed in Great Britain by C. I. Thomas & Sons (Haverfordwest) Ltd, Press Buildings, Merlins Bridge, Haverfordwest.

(Opposite) John Vanbrugh: a portrait by Sir Godfrey Kneller painted between 1704 and 1710.

The Temple of the Winds, Vanbrugh's last contribution to Castle Howard, 1724-6, and completed after his death.

Arms and the stage

EARLY LIFE

John Vanbrugh was born in January 1664, being christened on the 24th of that month in his father's house in London. His father, Giles Vanbrugh, owned a sugar-refining business and seems to have been moderately rich. His grandfather was Giles Van Brugg, a Protestant merchant of Ghent who had fled to London to escape persecution and married an Englishwoman.

John's father prospered sufficiently to marry the daughter of Sir Dudley Carleton, nephew and heir to Lord Dorchester. John was the fourth of their nineteen children but the eldest son to survive childhood. He was proud of his ancestry and in later life claimed descent from a Praetor of Ypres in 1483.

Before John was three years old the family moved to Chester, possibly as a consequence of the Great Plague of London in 1665. Here the sugar-refining continued, their house being known as the Sugar House, and here presumably John went to school, but little more is known of his early life.

THE SOLDIER

At the age of twenty-two he received a commission in the Earl of Huntingdon's regiment of foot, but he resigned a few months later to avoid the tediousness of garrison duty in Guernsey. On the death of his father in 1689 he came into a modest income and in 1690 he appears at Calais where he was arrested whilst sketching the fortifications, according to one version of the story. If we are to believe another version, his arrest was at the instance of a woman who reported that he had left Paris without a passport whilst France and England were at war. But there is little doubt that he was, in fact, spying. At all events he was imprisoned, first at Calais, then at Vincennes, and early in 1691 he was moved again, on the orders of Louis XIV, to the Bastille in

Paris. His time in the Bastille was not especially arduous as will be seen from subsequent events.

In November 1692 he was suddenly paroled and allowed to return home. The reason for this improvement in his fortunes never became clear, any more than the reason for his arrest or indeed the precise nature of his activities in France. His release was probably part of a complex bartering of prisoners such as was common at the time.

A brief period in a minor post in the royal household followed. Then he seems to have joined the Marines and in 1696 was commissioned in Lord Berkeley's Marine Regiment of Foot and served until the regiment was disbanded in 1698. He had resumed his connection with the Earl of Huntingdon's regiment by 1702, when he was commissioned captain, but he resigned almost at once as a new field of activity opened for him as Comptroller of the Works.

By this time he liked to be known as Captain Vanbrugh or Vanbrook, his own spelling of his name being variable. There was a vague suggestion that he was a veteran soldier of Marlborough's wars, although as far as is known he was never seriously engaged in any war.

THE DRAMATIST

During his imprisonment in the Bastille Vanbrugh does not appear to have found conditions so uncomfortable as to preclude his passing the time in drafting a comedy. This seems to have been his first attempt in a form of activity in which he was destined to make his mark.

The period during which Vanbrugh wrote his plays was a time of constant disputes between theatres and the companies which appeared in them. In 1695 there was a quarrel between the patentees of the Theatre Royal, Drury Lane, and Thomas Betterton, the outstanding actor of the time. Betterton withdrew, along with some of the other senior members of the company, and moved to the rival new theatre in Lincoln's Inn Fields. The remainder of the company endeavoured to carry on at Drury Lane and Colley Cibber, hitherto known only as an actor, turned playwright with *Love's Last Shift,* a comedy produced in 1696. This inspired Vanbrugh to set to work hurriedly to write a sequel, which was produced as *The Relapse or Virtue in Danger.* The play was the sensation of the following season and Vanbrugh was firmly launched as a writer for the stage. In the prologue he writes that it was 'got, conciev'd, and born in six weeks' space'.

His second work for the stage was notably less successful. This was *Aesop,* a two-part free translation and adaptation from the French of Boursault's *Esope.* Produced in 1697, the prologue admits that it contains:

> 'No Hero, no Romance, no Plot, no Show,
> No Rape, no Bawdy, no Intrigue, no Beau'.

The public took him at his word and its success was very moderate.

Vanbrugh next completed the play he had commenced in the Bastille with the title *The Provok'd Wife* but went over to Betterton's company at the Lincoln's Inn Fields theatre. The play was a great success at its first performance in 1697 but brought Vanbrugh notoriety as well as fame.

ATTACK BY COLLIER

The Relapse and *The Provok'd Wife* delighted a majority of the play-going public but caused offence to the puritan element in society by their undoubted bawdiness and indecencies. In 1698 Jeremy Collier issued *A Short View of the Immorality and Profaneness of the English Stage.*

Collier was a clergyman, a lecturer of Gray's Inn, London, and eventually a non-juring bishop. Officially he was an outlaw, having been involved in scaffold benedictions at the execution of Jacobites. He was almost a professional controversialist and his attack on the morality of the stage was but the most famous of a series of such campaigns. The history of the English theatre is a series of swings towards immorality and compensating swings back to more puritanical standards. Collier's attack undoubtedly caused the pendulum to swing in the latter direction for some years.

Vanbrugh seems to have anticipated such an attack, and indeed the direction from which it would come. In the preface to *The Relapse* he writes of '. . . any man (with flat plod shoes, a little band, greasy hair, and a dirty face, who is wiser than I at the expense of being forty years older) . . .'. The challenge was duly taken up and Vanbrugh along with Congreve and Farquhar figured prominently in the *Short View.*

Collier held that 'the business of plays is to recommend virtue and discountenance vice' and upon this arguable hypothesis he charged Vanbrugh with bawdiness and blasphemy. Of the first charge Vanbrugh must certainly be convicted in some degree but his plays stand in a long tradition of bawdiness stretching back at least to

Shakespeare. The blasphemous element in Vanbrugh's plays is present in much smaller degree. He never had much liking for clergy of any persuasion, thinking them riddled with hypocrisy, and he had more reason for these beliefs in his time than there has been at most others.

Collier singled out Congreve and Vanbrugh for attack. Congreve was prosecuted and Betterton and Mrs Bracegirdle, who had played two of the leads in *The Provok'd Wife,* were fined, but the futility of the attack is shown by the continued success of this type of play.

Vanbrugh was genuinely surprised when he was accused of immorality and blasphemy in his plays. He was the least intellectual of playwrights and it probably never occurred to him to analyse what he was writing.

Later in 1698 he counter-attacked with *A Short Vindication of 'The Relapse' and 'The Provok'd Wife' from Immorality and Profaneness* but made the mistake of fighting Collier on his own ground rather than questioning the basis of his attack. It is a rather lame performance; indeed, the preface to *The Relapse,* although written before Collier's attack, is a more convincing statement of his essentially moderate view of the matter. It is also much more entertaining.

The controversy with Collier did not prevent Vanbrugh from continuing his work in the theatre but it may well have served to change its direction. Henceforth, with one exception, he contented himself with adaptations and translations from French plays. The exception was *A Journey to London,* unfinished at his death, and which cannot be dated but was presumably his last work in the medium. It was completed and adapted by Colley Cibber in 1728 and as *The Provok'd Husband* was popular throughout the remainder of the century.

VANBRUGH AND THE PLAY
The qualities which Vanbrugh contributed to English drama were vigour and common sense. He had a contempt for all cant and humbug. Yet he cannot be regarded as a serious poet because he lacked a distinctive outlook on life. His outlook was like that of his fellows and he could add little to the view of life common to most men of his time. The situations in his plays are the commonplace events in the society in

(Opposite) David Garrick in the character of Sir John Brute in 'The Provok'd Wife'. Painting by John Zoffany in the collection of the National Theatre.

The late Richard Wattis as Moneytrap, Dora Bryan as Clarissa, Frank Middlemass as Gripe and Jeannette Sterk as Araminta in 'The Confederacy' at the Chichester Festival Theatre, 1974. The play was written by Vanbrugh in 1705.

which he moved and it is these situations which hold our interest. He made no attempt to enlarge the vision of his audience and the contrast with the universality of the great masters of drama could hardly be more complete.

The speech of his plays is the everyday speech of the fashionable society of his times, almost certainly written rapidly and easily. His dialogue has a modern ring even in the twentieth century.

If Vanbrugh as a playwright is not to be taken more seriously than he took himself, he was yet a considerable master of the stage. His plays are constructed around plots which hold our interest and it is the situations which are the main element in his drama. Some, at least, of his characters are mere pasteboard and even the principals sometimes have disconcerting discrepancies in their characterisation.

Vanbrugh once wrote that his only reason for writing a play was to divert the gentlemen of the town 'and make them forget their spleen in spite of their wives and taxes'. Much of his approach derives from the Elizabethan drama with its rumbustious vitality. All but two of his plays were adaptations and even these two are derivative from older writers. But originality is not an indispensable quality in drama and all playwrights depend to some degree upon their predecessors.

Vanbrugh was not a great playwright. In his day he was a popular one and today his plays can still amuse us and divert us for an hour or so. They are of interest too for the illumination they give of the manners of some sections of the society in which he lived. This is not a high assessment of Vanbrugh as a playwright. He himself would probably have been surprised that anyone should expect a higher.

Castles and palaces

CASTLE HOWARD

Vanbrugh had hardly commenced his career as a dramatist when he began another as an architect. The details of this surprising development have not been recorded but he must, at the very least, have been thinking about architecture for some time in view of the scale of his first architectural project. His contemporaries thought the transition so abrupt that Swift wrote:

'Van's genius, without thought or lecture,
Is hugely turned to architecture.'

At all events, in 1699 he produced his first designs for a great mansion for the Earl of Carlisle in Yorkshire at what was to become known as Castle Howard. Charles Howard, third Earl of Carlisle (1669-1738), belonged to the Kit Kat Club, where Vanbrugh was also a prominent member. The club was a gathering of Whigs which originally met at the house of Christopher Katt, a pastrycook who specialised in mutton pies which were called Kitt-cats.

Carlisle had already consulted William Talman about his new house. Talman had originated the grand manner in country-house design, the house being intended to impress the beholder with the grandeur of the conception as much as to accommodate the occupants.

Vanbrugh shared this new approach to designing a great house but thought he could design even more splendid layouts. The designs for Castle Howard evolved over a long period and through many drawings. They show an increasingly complex design, with the climax being built up from the low side wings to the cupola crowning the central block. Yet the cupola, which seems today to be so essential to the scheme, is not shown on drawings made even after work had commenced on the

(Opposite) The dramatic interior of the hall at Castle Howard lit from windows in the cupola.

13

The scheme for Castle Howard as published in 'Vitruvius Britannicus' in 1725. The wing and courtyard to the right and the foreground works were never constructed to this design.

lower stages. The whole approach was a new one in the diversity of the grouping of the parts of the composition and the building up to a dominating crescendo in the cupola. This was the quality later to be described as 'movement' in architecture, an indispensable feature of the baroque — not that either of these terms would have meant anything to Vanbrugh himself.

The design for Castle Howard is an astonishing first essay in architecture and was for a building then one of the largest houses in England. It would be quite incredible were it not for the fact that Vanbrugh had obtained the assistance of Nicholas Hawksmoor as a kind of coadjutor. Hawksmoor (1661-1736) had become 'domestic clerk' to Sir Christopher Wren at about eighteen years of age and by 1699 had all the technicalities of building on a large scale at his

14

command. He probably dealt with all the purely practical matters but in addition there seems no doubt that he contributed a major share in the total design process.

Building began in 1700. The house comprised a centre block containing a great hall with a very dramatic interior and lower side wings making a south front some 292 feet long and containing the state apartments. On either side there were to have been side wings enclosing a great forecourt, that on the east, comprising the private apartments, being completed by 1711. The west wing with the stables was never built, the house being completed after Vanbrugh's death to a quite different design.

The house is sited on a hilltop with fine views to north and south. Vanbrugh was among the earliest architects to take care to site his buildings in relation to fine views and the siting of a house in North Yorkshire on a hilltop provoked much comment at the time. Vanbrugh could argue that all the state rooms faced south, but the private rooms of the owner were in a courtyard facing due north. He was sensitive on the point and on the possibility of draughts through his long stone-vaulted corridors and high rooms. In October 1715, after Lord Carlisle had spent some time in the house in very cold weather, Vanbrugh wrote: 'My Lord Carlisle was pretty much under the same aprehensions . . . about long Passages, High Rooms &c. But he finds what I told him to be true. That those long Passages would be so far from gathering and drawing wind as he feared, that a Candle wou'd not flare in them. Of this he has lately had the proof, by bitter stormy nights in which not one Candle wanted to be put into a Lanthorn . . . He likewise finds that all his Rooms, with moderate fires Are Ovens . . .'

Long before his house was finished Carlisle began to be more interested in the layout of the park and its ornamentation by garden buildings. Vanbrugh was anxious to complete the house but Carlisle insisted on building a series of structures in the grounds. Many of these seem to have been designed by Hawksmoor but Vanbrugh was certainly responsible for the Temple of the Winds which now forms a foreground feature to the serene view across the park to the Mausoleum built by Hawksmoor after Vanbrugh's death. Also by Vanbrugh are the mock fortifications which punctuate the main approach to the house. A preoccupation with battlements and turrets is a recurring theme in the architecture of Vanbrugh. Here is one of the earliest examples of a

The cupola at Castle Howard seen from the hall below.

romantic feeling for the Middle Ages, a nostalgic harking back to the age of chivalry. Vanbrugh was a romanticist long before his time, although he certainly would not have applied such a term to himself or indeed understood it, for he was the least intellectualising of designers.

THE GOOSE PIE

In 1700 Vanbrugh began building himself a small house in London in what is now Whitehall Gardens, just to the north-east of Inigo Jones's Banqueting House. The site had been cleared in 1698 by a fire which had largely destroyed the old Tudor palace of Whitehall. The fact that he was allowed to use such a site for a private dwelling indicates that he had influential friends.

The building was subsequently much altered before it was finally demolished in 1898 but as first built it must have looked rather like a blockhouse. Contemporary opinion thought it very odd, all set among

The south front of Castle Howard: (above) an early study by Vanbrugh; (below) as it was built and appears today.

Vanbrugh

The Goose Pie House, built by Vanbrugh for himself, as seen in a lecture diagram by Sir John Soane.

the rubbish of the burned-out palace. Swift wrote in 1703:

> '... Now Poets from all quarters ran
> To see the house of brother Van:
> Look'd high and low, walk'd often round,
> But no such house was to be found:
> One asks the waterman hard by,
> "Where may the Poets' palace lie?"
> Another of the Thames inquires
> If he has seen its gilded spires?
> At length they in the rubbish spy
> A thing resembling a Goose-Pye . . .'

Not surprisingly Vanbrugh took offence when this was published and a long quarrel ensued.

COMPTROLLER OF THE WORKS

In June 1702 Vanbrugh was appointed Comptroller of the Works, the second post in the organisation responsible for government buildings. Appointments to such offices were frequently made on political grounds as much as on those of technical competence and Vanbrugh must have been chosen at least partly from political considerations. He made no secret of his Whig affiliations. His friend Lord Carlisle was now Lord Treasurer and it was doubtless to him that Vanbrugh owed his appointment.

The head of the Works organisation was the aging Sir Christopher Wren, whose clerk was Hawksmoor. Vanbrugh must have already known the latter for he was involved in the designs for Castle Howard from the beginning in 1699. The connection may have arisen through Vanbrugh's cousin, William Vanbrugh, who was secretary of Greenwich Hospital. The hospital was being built on the site of the former royal palace and as it was a royal building Wren and his clerk were responsible.

In 1703 a new board of directors for the hospital was appointed and this included Vanbrugh, who gradually played a more and more important role until he replaced Wren as surveyor in 1716. By then little further design work remained to be done and Hawksmoor was probably largely responsible for the buildings erected at Greenwich. Their design raises interesting questions, for they are quite unlike anything that Wren had ever designed. There is a wildness, even abandon, which may well have been due to Vanbrugh. Hawksmoor was to absorb this quality very thoroughly until he created works of a quite distinctive kind when there is no question of Vanbrugh being involved, as in his London churches. Yet it cannot be just absorption on the part of Hawksmoor, for some of the buildings at Greenwich were commenced in 1699, the same year as that in which Vanbrugh made his sudden appearance before the world as architect. Doubtless it was a two-way process and the evolution of Vanbrugh's personal style may well have been aided by Hawksmoor.

THE HERALD

Not content with being by now a playwright and an architect, Vanbrugh became Carlisle Herald Extraordinary in 1703 and the following year Clarenceux King of Arms, the former appointment being made to conform to a rule that a king of arms must have previously served as a herald. These were further fruits of his friendship with Lord Carlisle, who was acting as Earl Marshal during the minority of the Duke of Norfolk. They brought him a useful income for no great expenditure of energy. Vanbrugh had earlier expressed his utter contempt for heraldry and everything associated with it and had held it to ridicule in his plays.

Whilst he saw his appointment largely as a source of income he did in 1706 travel to Hanover to confer the Order of the Garter on the future King George II and later officiated as deputy to Garter King of Arms. His appointment caused great offence in the College of Arms but in spite of a petition from the pursuivants he was installed. That he regarded the office more as a piece of property than a duty is shown by the fact that shortly before his death he sold it for £2,400.

THE OPERA HOUSE

Vanbrugh was both playwright and architect and it was natural that he should think of combining these interests by building a theatre. In 1703 he paid £2,000 for a site in the Haymarket in London and proceeded to build a theatre of quite unprecedented magnificence. Unfortunately the acoustics were less splendid. Cibber wrote: '. . . what could their vast columns, their gilded cornices, their immoderate high roofs avail, where scarce one word in ten could be distinctly heard in it?'

The opera house brought Vanbrugh little but trouble. He had originally intended to manage the theatre with Congreve but the latter withdrew. He had hoped to put on Italian opera but the London public were not ready for it. Financial problems multiplied and may well have contributed to his withdrawal from the stage in 1705 when his last completed play was produced.

The Italian Opera House, as it became known, was extensively refitted in 1778 and destroyed by fire in 1789, but the site continued to be occupied by a theatre and Her Majesty's Theatre now stands where once Vanbrugh was embroiled in his worries.

BLENHEIM

On 13th August 1704 the armies of Louis XIV, hitherto regarded as invincible, were crushingly defeated at Blenheim, a village in Bavaria, by allied armies commanded by John Churchill, created Duke of

Blenheim Palace: the south facade of the main block with its corner towers crowned by martial plumes.

Marlborough for his services. But the gratitude of a grateful nation did not stop at mere titles. Queen Anne was a close personal friend of the Duke and Duchess and she presented them with Woodstock Park in Oxfordshire in which a house of dimensions suitable to the occasion would be built and paid for from the royal purse.

The details of these arrangements were vague but it hardly seemed to matter since Marlborough was the hero of half Europe and in the highest favour with his queen.

As this was to some extent a royal building it was natural that the Office of Works should be involved. One story suggests that Wren, as Surveyor of the Works, had suggested his deputy Vanbrugh for the new house. Later the Duchess said that Queen Anne had appointed Vanbrugh. He himself said that the Duke had offered him the job at a casual meeting in the playhouse in Drury Lane. At all events he took the precaution of getting a warrant of appointment drawn up and endorsed by Lord Godolphin, the Lord Treasurer, who acted for Marlborough when he had returned to the wars. As events were to prove this was a wise precaution.

Shortly afterwards the Duke and Lord Treasurer Godolphin called at Vanbrugh's house in Whitehall to discuss the design. Vanbrugh had a model of Castle Howard and the Duke indicated that that was the sort of house he wanted, with a few alterations and additions. As in the case of Castle Howard the invaluable Hawksmoor was engaged to assist.

There had long been a manor-house in Woodstock Park. Although it was in poor condition Vanbrugh thought it still habitable. It appealed to the romantic in him and he proposed to build his palace on the other side of the river Glyme which flows across the park leaving the old manor as an agreeable incident in the view from the new building. He wrote that the old manor would make 'One of the Most Agreeable Objects that the best of Landskip Painters could invent'. Later he used the building as quarters for himself during his stays at Blenheim, to the great annoyance of the formidable Duchess.

As sited by Vanbrugh, the main axial approach was from the north across the marshy valley of the little river. To carry the awestruck visitor across, Vanbrugh designed an enormous bridge. The cost of this extravagance further infuriated the Duchess although the Duke undoubtedly had a liking for the expansive ideas of his architect. The Duchess complained that there were thirty-three rooms in the bridge. The river beneath was dragooned into a series of formal pools that were quite inadequate in scale with the bridge. Pope's comment was typical of that of many visitors:

'The minnows, as under this vast arch they pass,
Murmur, "How like whales we look, thanks to your Grace".'

Horace Walpole wrote that the bridge was 'Like the beggars at the old Duchesses gate, it begged for a drop of water and was refused.' Yet the bridge is among the finest things Vanbrugh ever did. The scale is gigantic and as designed it was to have carried a superstructure, omitted at the insistence of the enraged Duchess.

The vast scale of palace and bridge called for a quite new type of setting. Vanbrugh in his initial siting and in the diffuse grouping of the buildings was reflecting ideas which were only just stirring among a few advanced thinkers. They saw the setting of a great house as an exercise in creating a picture in terms of real scenery. Forty years later, when these ideas had developed into the English landscape movement, the leading exponent, Lancelot 'Capability' Brown, came to Blenheim and by damming up the river created a lake which flooded the lower levels of Vanbrugh's bridge but which provided the great sheet of water needed to be in scale. Palace and bridge are now seen in a setting Vanbrugh could not have envisaged himself but of which he would

The great bridge at Blenheim, cause of so much friction between Vanbrugh and the Duchess of Marlborough. Two storeys are now beneath water level and a superstructure intended by Vanbrugh was never added.

surely have approved, for it is one of the supreme designed landscapes of the world. The whole seems entirely appropriate and indeed inevitable for Vanbrugh and Brown were working at different stages in the development of the same sequence of ideas.

Work on the palace proceeded rapidly, almost as rapidly as great victories added further glories to the name of Marlborough, but from 1707 relations with the Queen deteriorated swiftly. The Duke was dismissed as Captain General and the Duchess from court. Matters went so far that the Duke and Duchess found it prudent to remain abroad for two years. Inevitably payments from the Treasury for work at Blenheim slowed down and then stopped altogether. At least £45,000 was owed to the builders and from 1712 to 1714 the vast structure remained deserted. The arrangements whereby the Treasury paid for the work but the Duke gave orders had always been uncertain. Now they evaporated altogether.

Clock-tower above the arch to the kitchen court, Blenheim Palace. Above the columns British lions are savaging the cockerels of France.

THE WOODSTOCK LETTER

The town of Woodstock, just outside the park, had become a 'pocket borough' where the Duke of Marlborough's nominee was virtually certain of being elected to Parliament. During the general election of 1710 the vast debt owed to the builders, which indirectly affected the finances of the entire population, was felt to be imposing a severe strain on the loyalty of the electors. The Duke's agent raised £300 on his own initiative and distributed this in the right quarters, thereby saving the day. At the election of 1712 the situation was much more serious. The Duke, still out of royal favour, was travelling on the Continent in involuntary exile and, more to the point, the debt was still unpaid. The Duke's friends felt that some significant gesture was called for.

Vanbrugh suggested that some town improvements might be carried out at the Duke's expense. The Duke had agreed to this before his departure. Vanbrugh therefore wrote to the Mayor of Woodstock to indicate the intention of the Duke to pave the streets of the town. He added that the Duke would have done this long since 'but for the continual plague and bitter persecution he has most barbarously been followed with for two years past'. Thus the Comptroller of the Works, an office-holder under the Crown, was criticising the Tory government and as he was a renowned Whig his action was indiscreet at the very least.

None of this would have mattered greatly, the Mayor of Woodstock being a Whig, had Vanbrugh not carelessly addressed the letter to Major of Woodstock and the letter was delivered to a Mr Major who was a confirmed Tory. He sent a copy to the Tory Lord Treasurer, Lord Oxford. The result was that Vanbrugh was dismissed as Comptroller of the Works.

Vanbrugh wrote to the Duke of Marlborough of the attitude of Queen Anne: 'She said she had been under an obligation to me not to consent to it, but my behaviour had been such in writing that Letter to Woodstock, that now she had done with me — That was her expression.'

Vanbrugh could ill afford to lose the salary and the Duke seems to have paid him £200 per year to ease the loss, incurred so largely in his cause. The year 1713 was a low point in Vanbrugh's life but the paving of Woodstock was carried out although his estimate of £300 proved somewhat short of the final cost of £500.

RESIGNATION

In 1714 Queen Anne died and her Tory government was replaced by the Whig government of George I. The Marlboroughs returned from their travels and the Duke decided to resume work on Blenheim, but this time at his own expense. Vanbrugh and Hawksmoor resumed their work and building was under way again by the summer of 1716. But that same November Vanbrugh took an enraged departure, goaded by the violent criticism of the Duchess into a final break. He concluded his letter of resignation that he 'shou'd put a very great afront upon your understanding if I suppos'd it possible you cou'd mean any thing in earnest by them; but to put a Stop to my troubling you any more. You have your end, Madam, for I will never trouble you more Unless the Duke of Marlborough recovers so far, to shelter me from such intollerable Treatment.

'I shall in the meantime have this Concern on his account (for whom I shall ever retain the greatest Veneration), that your Grace having like the Queen thought fit to get rid of a faithful servant, the Torys will have the pleasure to See your Glassmaker Moor make just such an end of the Duke's Building as her Minister Harley did of his Victories for which it was erected.'

James Moor, who was by origin a cabinet-maker rather than a glassmaker, took over the direction of operations at Blenheim until after the death of the Duke. Later Hawksmoor returned and added several of the park buildings and some interiors, but Vanbrugh had gone forever. Years later, in 1725, he was in a party with Lord Carlisle visiting Woodstock. At the entrance to the park the gatekeeper showed them an order 'under her Grace's own hand' not to admit him. Whilst the rest of the party went to see the palace its designer went to Old Woodstock and looked over the park wall to see his great building on its hill in the distance.

(Opposite) Portrait of Sir John Vanbrugh attributed to T. Murray, about 1718.

(Above) Kimbolton Castle. The south wing seen here was rebuilt by Vanbrugh in 1707-10. Note the battlements and 'Masculine Shew'.

(Below) Kings Weston, Avon. The south front showing the remarkable arcaded chimney feature which has recently been restored.

Battlements and turrets

KIMBOLTON CASTLE

Kimbolton Castle, near Huntingdon, was a late seventeenth-century adaptation of a Tudor manor-house. Which architect was responsible for the adaptations is uncertain but it may have been William Coleman, a joiner by origin. In the summer of 1707 the south range of the quadrangular building collapsed and after Coleman had prepared some designs for rebuilding which cannot have been found satisfactory by the owner, the fourth Earl of Manchester, he sent for his fellow Kit Kat Club member, Vanbrugh.

The Earl was ambassador in Venice at the time and Vanbrugh had to send his sketches to Venice explaining the plainness of the exterior proposed: 'As to the Outside I thought 'twas absolutely best, to give it something of the Castle air, tho' at the Same time to make it regular. And by this means too all Old Stone is serviceable again; which to have had new wou'd have run to a very great expense . . . I hope your Ldship wont be discourag'd, if any Italians you may Shew it to, shou'd find fault that 'tis not Roman, for to have built a Front with Pillasters, and what the Orders require cou'd never have been borne with the Rest of the Castle; I'm sure this will make a very Noble and Masculine Shew; and is as Warrantable a kind of building as Any.'

Coleman acted as clerk of works and earned Vanbrugh's unstinted praise for his work: 'I have a Constant Correspondence with Coleman, and am in most things very well satisfy'd with him; If we had Such a Man at Blenheim, he'd save us a Thousand pounds a Year.' For his part Coleman wrote of Vanbrugh: 'If their is aney Credit Gayned In this Bulden, I beg that he may have it.'

Having completed the rebuilding of the collapsed south wing, the builders went on to reface the other three sides. The work included the provision of battlements along the top of each facade, another reminder of Vanbrugh's love of hints of medievalism in architecture.

On the east front a great portico was added, probably also by Vanbrugh, and there is in existence a Gothic design for this although it was not executed.

CLAREMONT

In 1708 Vanbrugh bought a site for a house for himself near Esher in Surrey. His mother had spent her early life nearby and, after the death of her sugar-refining husband, returned to the area. Vanbrugh's house was a modest affair but suited to a romantic site. In spite of its small size the house had corner turrets and battlements and within were the vaulted corridors so characteristic of his great houses.

In 1711 his mother died and almost at once he seems to have sold his house to Thomas Pelham-Holles, then eighteen years old and destined to become successively Lord Pelham, Earl of Clare and Duke of Newcastle. He was to be a good friend to Vanbrugh and was one of the Whig circle in which Vanbrugh found almost all of his friends. One manifestation of Pelham-Holles's friendship may well have been to purchase Vanbrugh's little country house for the latter was severely short of money at this time.

By 1715 Vanbrugh had commenced enlargements for the new owner by building wings either side, leaving a courtyard in front. Within the east wing was a 'great room', the biggest he ever designed for a private house and so high as seriously to disturb the symmetry of the whole composition. In the midst of all this splendour Vanbrugh's little house was refitted as far as possible for its new role by being equipped with pediments in place of battlements.

In the grounds a tall brick belvedere tower was built in 1717 with angle towers and battlements and great arched windows to the lower storeys. The general effect is vaguely medieval and extremely picturesque; indeed, the very idea of a tower built for no other purpose than a place from which to admire the view is wholly picturesque. The Claremont belvedere is an astonishingly early instance of a mode of thought which was destined to play a major role in English art.

The walled gardens and gardeners' houses date from after 1723 and display the characteristic heaviness in brickwork and arches of their designer, as do the battered rectangular bastions.

KINGS WESTON

In 1710 Sir Edward Southwell, Secretary for Ireland, MP for Rye

(Above) A sketch showing Vanbrugh's own small country house near Esher, Surrey, as it appeared before 1715.

(Right) The belvedere tower at Claremont, Esher, as it survives today.

(Below) Claremont as expanded by Vanbrugh for the Duke of Newcastle. His own small house can still be seen in the centre with its battlements replaced by pediments. The 'Great Room' is on the right and the belvedere tower can be seen in the left background. An engraving by Roque, 1738.

31

and a friend of Swift, engaged Vanbrugh to rebuild the house near Bristol which he had inherited. The main structure was completed by 1714 although work continued for many years on fittings and garden buildings. Kings Weston shows well how Vanbrugh could take advantage of a spectacular site, here overlooking the Severn estuary.

The main front has a massive engaged portico and within much space is taken up by a splendid hanging staircase supported only from the walls. Here too are Vanbrugh's favourite arcaded walls with niches containing painted statues and urns. But the outstanding feature of the house is undoubtedly the roofline. The rows of chimneys are connected by arches so that there are arcades on the roof on the three main facades. The effect of this is to raise the centre of the house with a vaguely castellated appearance. Vanbrugh took great care over this feature, writing to the owner not to commence work from the drawings only, but to wait until he could attend himself '. . . to make tryall of the heights etc, with boards . . . I would fain have that part rightly hit off' — an interesting glimpse into his methods of executing his buildings.

STOWE

Another of Vanbrugh's Whig friends was Richard Temple, later to be Viscount Cobham, who had served as an officer under Marlborough. Like his general he was out of royal favour between 1710 and 1714 and used his enforced leisure to carry out improvements at his estate at Stowe near Buckingham.

He concentrated on the gardens around his late seventeenth-century house and engaged Charles Bridgeman as garden designer. The art of garden design was, under Bridgeman's leadership, just taking the first hesitant steps away from the symmetrical, formal layouts of the past and along the path that was to lead to the landscape gardens of the latter half of the eighteenth century.

Vanbrugh was engaged to design the buildings with which the new grounds were liberally embellished and also carried out some work on the house in an endeavour to increase its apparent consequence as seen from the developing landscape around. To what extent Vanbrugh was involved in the design of this landscape itself is far from clear. He was much interested in the relationship between building and landscape elsewhere and his memorandum of 1709 about the desirability of preserving the old Woodstock Manor as a picturesque element in the landscape is among the earliest evidences of concern for the preservation of an old building. It seems impossible that he should not have had considerable influence on Bridgeman in evolving a new kind of landscape design in which buildings were designed to be seen from many angles, with all kinds of cross views between them, instead of the single vistas of the old formal layouts.

The works at Stowe involved the creation of a wide central glade down to an octagonal lake, all largely symmetrical, but otherwise the grounds were quite asymmetrical with curving paths and other then unconventional devices. Such a garden was intended to evoke suitably romantic thoughts in the observer and to this end buildings of suitable form and assisted by suitably evocative inscriptions were essential.

Buildings by Vanbrugh which remain in the grounds include the Lake Pavilions of 1719 and the Rotunda of much the same date, both altered later. Now gone are the Egyptian pyramid, a guilio or rusticated obelisk once in the centre of the octagonal lake, a Temple of Bacchus, Dido's Cave, a Sleeping Parlour, Nelson's Seat and a Bagno. Beyond the grounds proper there still remains the Bourbon Tower, a curious structure of ironstone which is another example of conscious medievalising on the part of Vanbrugh.

After his death his work at Stowe was commemorated with an inscription on his pyramid and Gilbert West wrote:

'The pointed Pyramid. This too is thine,
Lamented Vanbrugh! This thy last Design,
Among the various structures that around
Form'd by thy Hand, adorn the happy ground,
This sacred to thy Memory shall stand:
Cobham and grateful Friendship so command.'

VANBRUGH CASTLE

Having sold his country home at Esher, Vanbrugh at length looked for a new one and, with the improvement in his fortunes consequent on the Whigs' return to power in 1714, he embarked upon a small development scheme on his own account.

In 1715 he had succeeded Wren as surveyor to Greenwich Hospital, so it was natural that he should look to that area for a site. About 1717 he bought land on the east side of Greenwich Park on Maze Hill with wide views across the valley. On this triangular-shaped piece of land he

Eastbury, Dorset. The remaining building is merely the stable wing on the north side of the forecourt of the original house.

built twelve or fifteen houses on what became known as Vanbrugh Fields.

The entrance was marked with characteristic emphasis by a brick archway. Beyond was a winding drive between the asymmetrically placed houses. The scheme included a house long known as The Nunnery for his brother Captain Charles and another for his brother Philip, also a captain in the Navy, which acquired the nickname of Mince Pie House. At the end of the drive one came to the climax of the visual experience with Vanbrugh's own house, Vanbrugh Castle, sited on the edge of Maze Hill to take full advantage of the views to the north over shipping in the Thames and his hospital on its banks.

All the houses seem to have been essays in the embattled manner that Vanbrugh considered suitable for small houses which he yet wished to appear to be of some consequence. Only his own house remains of this scheme, set now in a commonplace street layout of later houses, but it conveys, with its turrets and battlements, the romantic feeling so loved by its designer. Within there are no large rooms but bow windows to take full advantage of the prospects and his favourite vaulted corridors. All the main rooms face north for the view, but Vanbrugh was never inclined to neglect a good view merely because the rooms never had any sunshine. The whole feeling of the building is medieval and Vanbrugh sometimes called it Bastille House in remembrance of the days he spent in another castle, yet there are no specifically medieval features. Today most passers by would dismiss the building as obviously Victorian, yet the symmetry of the facade is of the age of Vanbrugh, not Victoria.

THE ORDNANCE

With the accession of George I in 1714 the Duke of Marlborough regained his position as Captain-General of the Forces and became even more influential than he had ever been under Queen Anne. Due to his influence Vanbrugh was given the first knighthood of the new reign. Earlier the Duke had promised him 'something substantial' for his services. In the event the knighthood was to prove to be all he was to get, although a little later he was restored to his old post of Comptroller of the Works. Due partly to the very fact of the Hanoverian succession, the government became seriously alarmed at the risk of invasion. The Office of Works was consequently involved in much work on military and naval defence building and Vanbrugh seems to have been closely concerned.

Documentary evidence is lacking but the style of many of the Ordnance buildings of the period leaves no doubt that if those buildings were not designed by Vanbrugh himself they were designed by someone very greatly under his influence. He may well have produced a general design leaving the detailed execution to subordinates on the spot. Hawksmoor was probably involved too.

EASTBURY

In 1716 Vanbrugh prepared designs for a great house in Dorset for George Dodington, a *nouveau riche*. Further designs were made in 1718 but Dodington died in 1720, leaving his estate to George Bubb, his nephew, son of a Weymouth apothecary, together with £30,000 to complete the house. Bubb gratefully changed his name to Bubb Dodington.

The house represents a further development of the forecourt theme as begun at Castle Howard and continued at Blenheim. Here the forecourt was almost two hundred feet wide with on either side an arcade, incorporated in which were a stable block and yard on one side and a kitchen wing on the other.

Contrary to his usual practice Eastbury was built with the wings before the main block. Even when the wings had been completed Vanbrugh was still revising his design for the centre. At one stage the block was to have been lower and wider, then it was narrowed, and extra arcades had to be built to link up with the side arcades which had already been built.

Eastbury was Vanbrugh's third largest house and by the time of its completion had cost £140,000, twice the cost of Castle Howard. Bubb Dodington became a highly flamboyant character under the influence of his wealth. When all was finished a description reads: 'The interior of his mansion was as proud and splendid as the exterior was bold and imposing. All this was exactly in unison with the taste of the magnificent owner, who had gilt and furnished the apartments with a profusion of finery that kept no terms with simplicity, and not always with elegance or harmony of style.'

Dodington died in 1762 as Lord Melcombe of Melcombe Regis, and thereafter his great house proved unattractive to any future grandee. In 1775 the central block was blown up and the south wing demolished. Today only the stable court and north side of the forecourt remain, patched up into a house of more reasonable dimensions. Being intended as a subordinate part of a more magnificent whole the remaining part exhibits Vanbrugh's blockish severity to an especial degree. Mouldings are just blocked in and the great cube rising above the severe lines of the arcade makes few concessions to elegance. The arch to the stable court survives, with two pine trees growing from the top, and beyond are traces of the vast formal gardens devised by Bridgeman. But the magnificence of the Dodingtons was short-lived indeed.

SEATON DELAVAL

In 1717 Admiral George Delaval bought the old house at Seaton, Northumberland, from an older branch of the family and wrote to his

Seaton Delaval, Northumberland: (above) the approach to the forecourt, with the stable block to the left and the private apartments to the right; (below) the impressive accommodation for horses.

brother: 'I intend to persuade Sir John Vanbrugh to see Seaton if possible & give me a plan of a house, or to alter the old one, which he is most excellent at; and if he cannot come, he'll recommend a man at York who understands these matters. So something may be done by degrees & be the entertainment of our old age or as long as we can live. I am much out of order with the scurvy.'

Vanbrugh did take on the commission and records that he first saw the site in bad weather. The climatic conditions must have further heightened the dramatic situation within a mile of the sea on a low, windswept hill facing north. The design is in many ways the culmination of his forecourt plans. Here the forecourt is enormous, 180 feet long and 152 feet wide, and open to the north with a distant view of Lindisfarne. On either side are long arcaded wings, the centre of each containing the stables and domestic quarters respectively. The central block, the climax of all this grandeur, is of surprisingly modest dimensions but easily compensates for lack of bulk by skilful grouping of masses. There are Vanbrugh's favourite corner turrets, here octagonal and almost detached from the main block, and square staircase towers are attached to each side and rise above roof level.

There is a marked distinction in character between the northern entrance front, with its almost frantic piling of mass on mass, and the southern garden front, which shows a little of the serenity of the Palladian movement which was to dominate English architecture later in the century. The great portico is almost elegant, a description which would certainly not fit the other facade.

For a site so far north Vanbrugh had to work largely through a clerk of works, William Etty of York. Even he must have been present only intermittently as he was acting in the same capacity at Castle Howard. Much was left to the agent, Mewburn, who, though well intentioned, was quite ignorant of architecture. He loathed Etty and once wrote: 'The groyning which Mr Etty mentions in his Letter, I think is a terme of Art, which is Arching of the Passage, as I apprehend him.'

The admiral was entirely behind the grandiose visions of his architect and the latter wrote: 'The Admiral is very Gallant in his operations, not being dispos'd to starve the Design at all.' Alas, long before his house was complete, the Admiral fell from his horse and was killed. Vanbrugh saw the house twice during construction but he too was dead before it was finished and misfortune seems ever since to have dogged the great house. The main block was later gutted by fire and today the owner, with a gallantry equal to that of his ancestor the admiral, is endeavouring to restore Seaton to something like its former glories.

ADAPTATIONS

During his architectural career Vanbrugh carried out many adaptations and improvements to old houses whose owners felt the need for something of 'more State and grandeur'. Thus he seems to have carried out a scheme at Audley End, Essex, where the main staircase in the hall and the accompanying screen are probably by him. Also associated with this work is a ceiling carefully designed to conform to the Jacobean decoration all around, another early instance of architectural revivalism.

In 1721 Vanbrugh visited Lumley Castle, County Durham, where Lord Lumley, later Lord Scarbrough, another Whig, had asked him to advise on improvements to his medieval castle. He wrote: 'Lumley Castle is a Noble thing; and well deserves the Favours Lord Lumley designs to bestow upon it; In order to which, I stay'd there near a Week, to form a General Design for the whole, Which consists in altering the House both for State, Beauty and Convenience.' The order of precedence of these qualities could hardly be more characteristic of Vanbrugh.

New state rooms were formed within the ancient walls but his exterior alterations were limited to a new main door and approach steps and some new windows. The old corner towers and battlements were already to Vanbrugh's taste and he left them alone in this most restrained of his works.

GRIMSTHORPE

During 1718 Vanbrugh was asked by the Duke of Newcastle to try to persuade the Duke of Ancaster to help him in opposing the Occasional Conformity Bill in the House of Lords. On the way to spend Christmas at Castle Howard he stopped at Ancaster's house, Grimsthorpe Castle in Lincolnshire, and, succeeding in his political aims, also succeeded in persuading the Duke to rebuild his castle.

There is evidence to suggest that Vanbrugh had previously worked for the Duke and built a large house at Swinstead on the Grimsthorpe estate. Little is known of this house but it would seem to have been of the Kings Weston type. Fragments still remain on the site and there is a massive doorway attached to a cottage. Nearby is a garden building which may well be by Vanbrugh.

He prepared designs for rebuilding Grimsthorpe during 1722 but the following year the Duke died. Vanbrugh wrote: '. . . but shall wait upon my new Grace of Ancaster in my way, having the honour of an invitation from him, to consult about his building; by which I believe he is inclined to go upon the general design I made for his Father last Winter and which was approved of by himself.' The plans were

(Above) The forecourt at Grimsthorpe Castle, Lincolnshire, with the hall in the centre of the north front. The double arcades reflect the design of the interior of the hall.

(Opposite) Finest of all Vanbrugh's interiors, the hall at Grimsthorpe Castle. Beyond the double stone screens can be seen the double staircase rising to the state dining room.

published in *Vitruvius Britannicus* in 1725 and included a large portico on the south front of a very Palladian type for Vanbrugh.

Work proceeded at Grimsthorpe from 1723 and comprised a north wing which was largely occupied by an enormous hall. On either side are attached towers containing a state dining room on one side and a chapel on the other. Before the facade is a large forecourt formed by arcaded walls leading to two-storey pavilions. The fourth side is closed by railings and a gateway of wrought iron. Through the park one approaches all this magnificence along an avenue aligned on the centre of the facade. Unlike Vanbrugh's other great houses Grimsthorpe has no central culmination, but the composition has a repose which is lacking from his earlier works. Within the exterior is reflected by the rows of blank and glazed arches. The outside is a logical expression of the interior, a quality so often missing in his other work. The hall at Grimsthorpe is the finest of all Vanbrugh interiors and the arched openings at either end screening double staircases are particularly impressive in spite of being tucked into a very small space.

On Vanbrugh's death all work ceased at Grimsthorpe and today his north range forms part of a quadrangle of otherwise Tudor and nineteenth-century work.

MARRIAGE

Vanbrugh spent Christmas of 1718 at Castle Howard. He wrote to the Duke of Newcastle: 'There has fallen a Snow up to one's Neck . . . In short 'tis so bloody cold, I have almost a mind to Marry to keep myself warm . . .'

This was the first hint to any of his friends that the bachelor of fifty-four was thinking of marrying a lady of twenty-five. She was Henrietta Maria Yarborough of Heslington Hall, York, and they were married in that city on 14th January 1719. It was a happy marriage and the home they made together was a great consolation in all the disappointments of his last years. There was political jobbery in the Office of Works where he was twice passed over for the senior office of Surveyor in favour of men of meagre talents. All his great houses save one had been designed but none had been completed. Yet he could write: 'I have a good humour'd wife, a quiet house, and find myself as much dispos'd to be a good friend and a servant as ever.'

There were money troubles. He had still not recovered from his losses in the Opera House venture and although the theatre was now flourishing he had let it on terms which brought him no profit. There were always the vexations over Blenheim and the wicked wiles of the Duchess pursuing her vendetta against him through the courts to the House of Lords. When that failed she opened a case in Chancery 'against every body that was ever concern'd in the Building of Blenheim downe to the poorest workman'. By the time the Duke of Marlborough died in 1722 Vanbrugh's admiration even for him had worn thin. He left over two million pounds 'And yet this man wou'd neither pay his Workmen their Bills nor his Architect his Salary. But he has given his Widdow (may a Scotch Ensign get her) £10,000 a Year, to Spoil Blenheim her own way, £12,000 a Year to keep her Self clean, and go to Law.'

LAST DAYS

At the last Vanbrugh managed to get at least some of the money owed to him from Blenheim by persuading the government to pay him

Part of a manuscript memorandum by Vanbrugh on the proposals to build fifty new churches in London in 1710. He proposed that no new burials be allowed in churches and that burial grounds be laid out on the edge of towns. His sketch shows one he had heard of. This is one of the few drawings indisputably in Vanbrugh's own hand.

out of the £30,000 which it had been agreed should be set aside to finish the royal gift of the palace. He wrote: 'Since being forc'd into Chancery, by that B.B.B.B. old B. the Dutchess of Marlbh., I say since my hands were tyed up, from trying by Law to recover my Arrear, I have prevailed with Sr. Rob. Walpole to help me in a Scheme I propos'd to him, by which I have got my money in Spight of the Huzzys teeth, and that out of a Sum, She expected to receive into her hands, and of which She resolv'd I should never have a farthing.'

In spite of this belated triumph his health began to deteriorate and he was often at Scarborough or Bath for his health. After 1723 this decline in health was pronounced and it was as much as he could do to

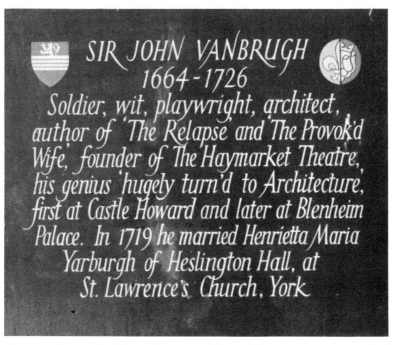

SIR JOHN VANBRUGH
1664-1726
Soldier, wit, playwright, architect,
author of 'The Relapse' and 'The Provok'd
Wife,' founder of 'The Haymarket Theatre,'
his genius 'hugely turn'd to Architecture,'
first at Castle Howard and later at Blenheim
Palace. In 1719 he married Henrietta Maria
Yarburgh of Heslington Hall, at
St. Lawrence's Church, York

Plaque at Vanbrugh College, University of York. The university has been built in the grounds of Heslington Hall, family home of Vanbrugh's wife.

go to the Office of Works. What he was suffering from is not clear but he describes 'blisters' and asthma. During March 1726 he developed quinsy, an acute form of tonsilitis which if not treated, and in the eighteenth century no effective form of treatment was known, leads to the impossibility of breathing. He died in his Goose Pie House in Whitehall on 26th March and five days later was buried beneath Wren's glorious dome of the church of Saint Stephen Walbrook in the tomb of his fathers.

Abel Evans provided the famous epitaph which is all that so many people know of Vanbrugh:

> 'Under this stone, Reader, survey
>   Dead Sir John Vanbrugh's house of clay.
> Lie heavy on him, Earth! for he
>   Laid many heavy loads on thee!'

IN THE FOOTSTEPS OF SIR JOHN VANBRUGH

Vanbrugh's greatest houses, Blenheim, Castle Howard and Seaton Delaval, are all open to the public regularly throughout the summer months. Grimsthorpe Castle is usually open to the public on two days each summer in aid of charities. Kings Weston is now a police training school and visitors should apply to the Chief Constable, Somerset and Avon Constabulary. The gardens at Stowe, now a school, are open daily during the school holidays. The post-Vanbrugh house at Claremont is now also a school but the grounds with the belvedere and kitchen garden walls can be seen on the first Saturday and following Sunday of each month, February to November. Lumley Castle is now a hotel and can be readily seen by patrons. Eastbury is not open to the public.

Robin Hood's Well, Skelbrooke, Yorkshire, reputed to have been designed by Vanbrugh for the Earl of Carlisle in 1711 and now standing near a layby on the Great North Road.

THE PRINCIPAL EVENTS OF VANBRUGH'S LIFE

1664 Vanbrugh born, 24th January, in London.
1686 Commissioned in the Earl of Huntingdon's Foot Regiment, 30th January. Resigned in August.
1689 Father dies leaving him a modest income.
1690 Arrested in Calais.
1692 Imprisoned in the Bastille. Drafts a comedy. Released in November and returns to England.
1696 Commissioned in Lord Berkeley's Marine Regiment of Foot. *The Relapse or Virtue in Danger* produced at Drury Lane.
1697 *Aesop, The Provok'd Wife* produced at Drury Lane. *The Country House.*
1698 Regiment disbanded.
1699 First designs for Castle Howard.
1700 *The Pilgrim.*
1701 Builds Goose Pie House in Whitehall for himself.
1702 *The False Friend.* Appointed comptroller of the Works. Captain in a new regiment of the Earl of Huntingdon, but left army shortly after.
1704 Becomes Clarenceaux King of Arms.
1705 *The Confederacy.* Appointed surveyor for Blenheim Palace. Opens the Opera House in the Haymarket, London.
1706 *The Mistake.* Sent to act as Garter King of Arms to invest future George II with Order of the Garter.
1707 Rebuilding of Kimbolton Castle (to 1714).
1708 Builds country home for himself near Esher.
1711 Building of Kings Weston, Avon (to 1714).
1713 Dismissed as Comptroller of the Works. Alterations at Cholmondley, Cheshire.
1714 Knighted by George I. Reinstated as Comptroller of the Works.
1715 House near Esher sold to Earl of Clare and enlarged as Claremont.
1716 Becomes surveyor to Greenwich Hospital. Resigns as surveyor to Blenheim Palace. First designs for Eastbury, Dorset.
1717 Builds Vanbrugh Castle, Greenwich, for himself.
1719 Marries Henrietta Maria Yarborough at York.
1720 Begins Seaton Delaval, Northumberland.

1721 Alterations to Lumley Castle, Co. Durham.
1722 Rebuilding of Grimsthorpe Castle, Lincolnshire (to 1726).
1726 Dies in London, 26th March.

BIBLIOGRAPHY

Biographies
Masks and Facades. Madeleine Bingham. Allen & Unwin, 1974.
Largely concerned with Vanbrugh's personal life rather than his
works.
Sir John Vanbrugh, Architect and Dramatist: 1664-1726. Lawrence
Whistler. Cobden-Sanderson, 1938. The standard biography.

Architecture
English Country Houses, Baroque, 1685-1715. James Lees-Milne.
Country Life, 1970. Detailed, well illustrated accounts of all the
great houses of Vanbrugh.
Hawksmoor. Kerry Downes. Thames & Hudson, 1969. Discusses the
relationship between Vanbrugh and Hawksmoor besides the life of
Vanbrugh's faithful helper.
The Imagination of Vanbrugh and his Fellow Artists. Lawrence
Whistler. Batsford, 1954. Extended account of the architecture of
Vanbrugh in relation to that of his times.

Drama
Lectures on the English Comic Writers. William Hazlitt. 1819. Many
editions including Everyman's Library. Lecture IV deals with
Wycherley, Congreve, Vanbrugh and Farquhar.
Sir John Vanbrugh ('Writers and their Work' series. No. 197).
Bernard Harris. Longmans Green, 1967. Useful introduction.
Restoration Comedy. Bonamy Dobree. Oxford, 1924. Contains a
valuable chapter on Vanbrugh and Farquhar.
The Complete Works of Sir John Vanbrugh (four volumes). Ed.
Bonamy Dobree and Geoffrey Webb. 1927.
There are recent paperback editions of *The Relapse* and *The Provok'd
Wife* in 'The New Mermaids' series, edited by Bernard Harris and
James L. Smith respectively. Benn, 1971 and 1974.

47

INDEX

Page numbers in italic refer to illustrations